Classic
INDIAN

Classic
INDIAN

Easy, delicious and authentic recipes

FOREWORD BY
RAFI FERNANDEZ

HERMES HOUSE

This edition published by Hermes House
an imprint of Anness Publishing Limited
Hermes House, 88-89 Blackfriars Road, London SE1 8HA

© Anness Publishing Limited 1996, 2003

Publisher Joanna Lorenz
Managing Editor Linda Fraser
Cookery Editor Anne Hildyard
Designer Nigel Partridge
Illustrations Madeleine David
Photographers Edward Allwright, David Armstrong, Steve Baxter and Michael Michaels
Recipes Roz Denny, Rafi Fernandez, Sarah Gates, Shehzad Husain,
Deh-Ta Hsiung and Steven Wheeler
Food for photography Shehzad Husain, Wendy Lee and Steven Wheeler
Stylists Maria Kelly and Blake Minton
Jacket photography Amanda Heywood
Production Controller Joanna King

Printed and bound in Singapore

3 5 7 9 10 8 6 4

For all recipes, quantities are given in both metric and imperial measures, and, where appropriate,
measures are also given in standard cups and spoons. Follow one set, but not a mixture,
because they are not interchangeable.

Picture on frontispiece: Zefa Pictures Ltd.
Pictures on pages 7, 8 & 9: Michael Busselle

CONTENTS

FOREWORD

The birth of classic cuisine in my country can be traced to necessity – that great mother of invention. Early settlers, seeking some way of preserving their food, discovered a large family of ingredients which would not only fulfil that function, but would also promote good health and pep up the appetite. These amazing ingredients were spices. Blending them soon became an art form: achieving the perfect proportions played a very important role in the development of classic Indian dishes.

India is a vast country, and it is not surprising that regions have evolved their own dishes. My country's food reflects the heritage of its peoples, embracing historical developments, religious beliefs and cultural practices. India has been influenced by many countries, absorbing aspects of their cooking along with their culture, but the unifying factor is the way that fragrant herbs and spices are blended to create dishes that are flavoursome, intriguing and addictive.

Recipes are handed down from generation to generation, often learned not from books but passed by word of mouth. Curry (the word originates from the Tamil *kaari*) simply means gravy with extra ingredients like meat, poultry, fish, seafood, pulses and many different vegetables.

Although the first commercial curry powder was invented in Madras in the early part of the nineteenth century, this was largely for export to the UK. Indians prefer to combine their own herbs and spices. The blend, which may be wet or dry, is called masala, and is prepared fresh each day after the menu has been planned. It is this blending of masalas that is the magic of our cuisine – even the humble potato can be transformed in a host of ways depending on the combination of different spices used to make the masala.

This beautifully illustrated book contains some of India's finest classic dishes. The emphasis is on home-cooking at its best, and recipes include preparations that have hitherto been the jealously guarded preserve of professionals. I am proud that several of my recipes have been chosen for this collection and wish you good dining or "*Priti Bhojan!*"

RAFI FERNANDEZ

INTRODUCTION

Indian cooking is renowned for its use of spices, herbs and flavourings. The dishes of this great sub-continent range from mild creamy kormas to the fiery curries of Madras, but the common denominator is the blending of spices so that each single dish has a distinctive signature, be it subtle or strident.

Indian dishes, even sweetmeats, are seldom cooked without spices. Rubbed into meats, made into masalas (the dry mixes or pastes used for curries), or combined with cream, yogurt or coconut milk to make rich, smooth sauces, spices are essential to authentic Indian cooking. Try to buy whole spices and grind them yourself, as once spices are ground they lose their flavour and aroma in a relatively short time.

Many Indian dishes, especially those from the south, owe their

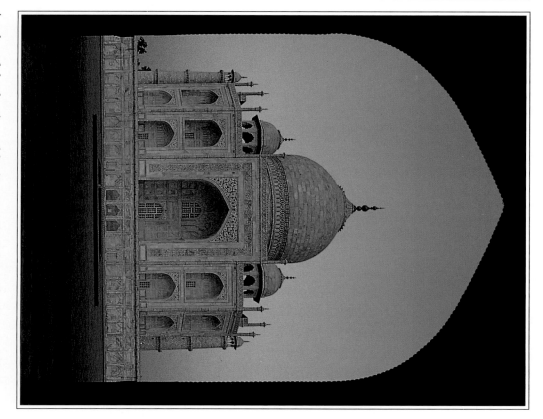

A colourful selection of fruit – an essential refreshment after spicy food (left), the breathtaking splendour of the Taj Mahal (above) and a stall selling a variety of sweet and savoury snacks (right), reflect some of the contrasting faces of India.

fiery flavour to fresh chillies. The seeds are particularly hot, and these may be discarded if you prefer a somewhat milder flavour. Use gloves when preparing chillies, or wash your hands very thoroughly afterwards. Touching delicate skin, especially around the eyes or lips, immediately after handling chillies, can cause an unpleasant reaction. Ginger also adds a hint of heat to many dishes. It is a very common ingredient in Indian cooking. Always use the fresh root ginger, rather than ground where this is indicated in recipes.

Other ingredients that frequently feature are fresh fruit and vegetables, dried pulses, rice and nuts. India has the largest population of vegetarians of any country in the world, and vegetables and grains are often presented as dishes in their own right. Ghee, which is a type of clarified butter, is also used extensively, especially in the north. It has a rich nutty flavour and is good for both shallow and deep-frying.

An Indian meal may consist of a meat or fish dish, one or two vegetable dishes, a dhal (a dish consisting of cooked pulses), a bowl of yogurt, bread and/or rice and perhaps a salad or a spicy chutney. Indian breads are the perfect vehicle for rich meat or fish dishes or dhals. However, bread is only served in northern, western and eastern India; in the south, rice is the more common accompaniment. There are countless ways of cooking rice, and each region adds some-

thing unique by way of flavouring. For everyday cooking, long grain or patna rice is used. When cooked, it should be dry and fluffy. For special dishes, basmati rice is favoured for its fine, delicately aromatic flavour. Indian meals often finish with fresh fruit such as mangoes or guavas. Alternatively, Kulfi, a delicious ice cream, is served (see page 56).

We are fortunate in being able to buy a wide range of spices and traditional Indian ingredients from our supermarkets and ethnic shops today. Whether your preference is for Tandoori Chicken, Lamb Korma, or Spiced Spinach and Potatoes, recreating *Classic Indian* dishes has never been easier, so invest in a few of your favourite spices, turn to any of the delectable recipes in this book, and treat your family and friends to the true taste of India.

9

CHICKEN TIKKA

This chicken dish is an extremely popular starter and is quick and easy to cook. It can also be served as a main course for four.

INGREDIENTS

450g/1lb skinless, boneless, chicken breast, cubed
5ml/1 tsp grated fresh root ginger
1 garlic clove, crushed
5ml/1 tsp chilli powder
1.5ml/¼ tsp ground turmeric
5ml/1 tsp salt
150ml/¼ pint/⅔ cup natural yogurt
60ml/4 tbsp lemon juice
15ml/1 tbsp chopped fresh coriander
15ml/1 tbsp vegetable oil
1 small onion, cut into rings, lime wedges, mixed salad and fresh coriander sprigs, to garnish

SERVES 6

COOK'S TIP

Serve Chicken Tikka, hot or cold, as a snack with drinks. Cut into bite-size pieces and serve on cocktail sticks.

1 In a bowl, mix together the chicken pieces, ginger, garlic, chilli powder, turmeric, salt, yogurt, lemon juice and coriander. Cover the bowl and leave to marinate for at least 2 hours.

2 Place the chicken pieces into a grill pan or a flameproof dish lined with foil and brush with the oil.

3 Preheat the grill to medium. Grill the chicken pieces for 15–20 minutes until cooked, turning and basting 2–3 times. Serve on individual plates, garnished with onion rings, lime wedges, mixed salad and fresh coriander sprigs.

SPICED AUBERGINES

The exact origins of the aubergine are uncertain but it has been cultivated in India since ancient times. It comes from the same family as the potato and is related to both the petunia and the tobacco plant.

INGREDIENTS

2 aubergines, halved lengthways

salt

60ml/4 tbsp olive oil, plus extra if needed

2 large onions, thinly sliced

2 garlic cloves, crushed

1 green pepper, seeded and sliced

400g/14oz can chopped tomatoes

40g/1½oz/3 tbsp sugar

5ml/1 tsp ground coriander

ground black pepper

30ml/2 tbsp chopped fresh coriander or parsley

fresh coriander sprigs, to garnish

crusty bread, to serve

SERVES 4

1 Using a sharp knife, slash the flesh of the aubergines a few times. Sprinkle with salt and drain in a colander for about 30 minutes. Rinse well and pat dry.

2 Gently fry the aubergines, cut-side down, in the oil for 5 minutes, then drain and place in a shallow ovenproof dish.

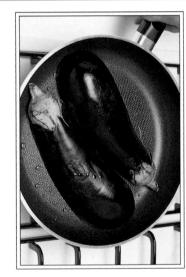

3 In the same pan, gently fry the onions, garlic and green pepper, adding extra oil if necessary. Cook for about 10 minutes, stirring occasionally, until all the vegetables have softened.

4 Add the tomatoes, sugar, ground coriander and black pepper to the onion and green pepper mixture. Stir to combine thoroughly, then cook for about 5 minutes until the mixture is reduced. Stir in the chopped coriander or parsley.

5 Preheat the oven to 190°C/375°F/Gas5. Spoon the mixture on top of the halved aubergines, cover and bake for 30–35 minutes. Cool, garnish with coriander sprigs, and serve cold with crusty bread.

COOK'S TIP

Sprinkling the cut surfaces of aubergines with salt allows the juices that form to drain away in a colander. Before cooking, it is important to rinse the aubergines well and pat dry with kitchen paper. Prepared like this, aubergines are less bitter.

SPICY KOFTA

S erve these tasty meatballs piping hot with naan bread, a raita made with cucumber and natural yogurt, tomato salad and a spicy relish.

INGREDIENTS

450g/1lb lean minced beef or lamb
30ml/2 tbsp grated fresh root ginger
2 garlic cloves, crushed
4 green chillies, finely chopped
1 small onion, finely chopped
1 egg
2.5ml/½ tsp ground turmeric
5ml/1 tsp garam masala
50g/2oz fresh coriander, chopped
4–6 fresh mint leaves, chopped, or
2.5ml/½ tsp mint sauce
1 potato, about 175g/6oz
salt
vegetable oil, for deep-frying

MAKES 20–25

1 Place the minced beef or lamb in a large bowl with the ginger, garlic, chillies, onion, egg, turmeric, garam masala, fresh coriander and mint or mint sauce. Grate the potato into the bowl and season with salt. Knead together to form a soft dough.

2 With your hands, shape the mixture into small patties the size of golf balls. Cover and leave to rest for about 25 minutes.

3 In a karahi or large frying pan, heat the oil to medium hot, add the meatballs in small batches and fry for 3–5 minutes until they are golden brown (*left*). Drain the meatballs well and serve immediately.

ONION BHAJIAS

 hajias are a classic Indian snack, like a fritter. The same batter may be used with a wide variety of vegetables, such as shredded carrots. Gram flour is a fine flour made from channa dhal. It is available from Indian shops,

INGREDIENTS

225g/8oz gram flour (besan) or
channa atta

2.5ml/½ tsp chilli powder

5ml/1 tsp ground turmeric

5ml/1 tsp baking powder

1.5ml/¼ tsp asafoetida

2.5ml/½ tsp each, nigella, fennel, cumin
and onion seeds, coarsely crushed

2 large onions, finely sliced

2 green chillies, seeded and chopped

50g/2oz fresh coriander, chopped

cold water, to mix

vegetable oil, for deep-frying

salt

MAKES 20–25

1 In a bowl, mix together the gram flour or *channa atta*, chilli powder and turmeric. Stir in the baking powder and asafoetida. Add salt to taste, then sift into a large mixing bowl.

2 Add the crushed nigella, fennel, cumin and onion seeds, the sliced onions, green chillies and fresh coriander and toss together well. Very gradually, mix in enough cold water to make a thick batter.

3 Heat enough oil in a karahi or large saucepan for deep-frying. Drop spoonfuls of the mixture into the hot oil and fry until golden brown. Leave enough space to turn the bhajias. Drain well and serve hot.

SAMOSAS

Traditional samosa pastry takes a lot of time and hard work but filo pastry makes an excellent substitute and is readily available. The samosas can be frozen before or after frying.

INGREDIENTS

1 packet filo pastry, thawed, if frozen, and wrapped in a damp dish towel
vegetable oil, for deep-frying

FOR THE FILLING

3 large potatoes, boiled and roughly mashed
75g/3oz/³⁄₄ cup frozen peas, boiled and drained
50g/2oz/¹⁄₃ cup canned sweetcorn, drained
5ml/1 tsp ground coriander
5ml/1 tsp ground cumin
5ml/1 tsp amchur (dry mango powder)
1 small red onion, finely chopped
2 green chillies, finely chopped
30ml/2 tbsp each chopped fresh coriander and mint
juice of 1 lemon, plus more if needed
salt
chilli sauce, to serve

MAKES 30

1 To make the filling, put the potatoes, peas, sweetcorn, ground coriander, cumin, amchur, onion, chillies, fresh coriander, mint, lemon juice and salt into a large mixing bowl and mix together until well blended. Taste and add more lemon juice and salt if necessary.

2 Using one strip of pastry at a time, place 15ml/1 tbsp of the filling mixture at one end. Diagonally fold up the pastry to form an enclosed triangle. Moisten the end of the strip with water; press lightly to secure.

3 Heat the oil in a karahi or large saucepan. Fry the samosas in small batches, turning frequently, until golden brown and crisp. Remove with a slotted spoon and drain on kitchen paper. Serve hot with chilli sauce.

VARIATION

To make a meat filling, fry 1 sliced onion in 30ml/2 tbsp oil for 5 minutes. Add 2 chopped garlic cloves, 15ml/1 tbsp each chopped fresh root ginger, ground cumin, ground coriander and salt and fry for about 1–2 minutes. Add 450g/1lb minced lamb and 45ml/3 tbsp water and brown. Cover the pan and cook for 20–25 minutes, stirring occasionally. Drain off the fat, stir in 30ml/2 tbsp chopped fresh mint, 1.5ml/¼ tsp garam masala and 15ml/1 tbsp lemon juice.

CHICKEN MULLIGATAWNY

T his hearty soup was originally made with *mulla ga tani* or pepper water, a sour, spicy flavouring mixture. It became very popular with the British in India during the days of the Raj. There are several variations.

INGREDIENTS

900g/2lb boneless, skinless chicken
breasts, cut into pieces
600ml/1 pint/2½ cups water
6 green cardamom pods
5cm/2in cinnamon stick
4–6 curry leaves
15ml/1 tbsp ground coriander
5ml/1 tsp ground cumin
2.5ml/½ tsp ground turmeric
3 garlic cloves, crushed
12 whole peppercorns
4 cloves
1 onion, finely chopped
115g/4oz creamed coconut
salt
juice of 2 lemons
deep-fried onions, to garnish

SERVES 4–6

1 Place the chicken pieces in a large saucepan with the measured water, bring to the boil, then cover and simmer for about 20 minutes, until the meat is tender. Skim the surface, then strain, reserving the stock. Set the chicken aside and keep warm.

2 Return the stock to the pan and bring back to the boil. Add all the remaining ingredients and simmer for 10–15 minutes, then strain and return the chicken to the soup. Reheat and serve garnished with the deep-fried onions.

18

TOMATO AND CORIANDER SOUP

A lthough soups are not often eaten in India and Pakistan, tomato soups of one kind or another are an exception. This one is excellent on a cold winter's day.

INGREDIENTS

675g/1½lb tomatoes
30ml/2 tbsp vegetable oil
1 bay leaf
4 spring onions, chopped
5ml/1 tsp salt
1 garlic clove, crushed
5ml/1 tsp black peppercorns, crushed
30ml/2 tbsp chopped fresh coriander
750ml/1¼ pints/3 cups water
15ml/1 tbsp cornflour
30ml/2 tbsp single cream, to garnish
(optional)
bread, to serve (optional)

SERVES 4

COOK'S TIP
Plum tomatoes are ideal for this recipe but if the only fresh tomatoes available are rather pale and under-ripe, add 15ml/1 tbsp tomato purée to the pan with the chopped tomatoes to enhance the colour and flavour of the soup.

1 To peel the tomatoes, plunge them into boiling water for 20–30 seconds, then into cold water. When cool, peel off the skins, then chop the tomatoes.

2 Heat the oil in a saucepan and fry the tomatoes, bay leaf and spring onions until soft. Add the salt, garlic, peppercorns and fresh coriander, and finally stir in the measured water. Bring to the boil, lower the heat and simmer for 15–20 minutes.

3 Mix the cornflour with a little water. Remove the soup from the heat and press through a sieve. Return to the pan, add the cornflour mixture and stir over a gentle heat for about 3 minutes until the soup is thickened and smooth.

4 To serve, ladle the soup into warmed individual bowls and garnish with a swirl of cream, if using. Serve immediately, with bread, if wished.

GRILLED FISH MASALA

These tasty fish fillets with their spicy coating are very simple to prepare. They are cooked using the minimum of oil, so are a healthy option.

INGREDIENTS

4 flat fish fillets, such as plaice, sole or flounder, about 115g/4oz each

SERVES 4

FOR THE SPICE MIXTURE
1 garlic clove, crushed
5ml/1 tsp garam masala
5ml/1 tsp chilli powder
1.5ml/¼ tsp ground turmeric
2.5ml/½ tsp salt
15ml/1 tbsp finely chopped
fresh coriander
15ml/1 tbsp vegetable oil
30ml/2 tbsp lemon juice
grated carrot, tomato quarters and
lime slices, to garnish

1 Line a flameproof dish or grill pan with foil. Rinse the fish fillets under cold running water, pat dry with kitchen paper and put them into the dish or pan.

2 To make the spice mixture, put the crushed garlic clove and garam masala into a small bowl. Stir in the chilli powder, ground turmeric, the salt and the finely chopped fresh coriander. Gradually add the vegetable oil, stirring constantly. Add the lemon juice and stir thoroughly to mix, then set the spice mixture aside. Preheat the grill to very hot.

3 Lower the temperature of the grill to medium. Using a pastry brush, baste the fish fillets evenly all over with the spice mixture. Grill the fish fillets on each side for about 5 minutes, basting occasionally with the juices that form in the pan, until they are cooked right through.

4 To serve, transfer the fish fillets to a warmed serving platter and make a decorative garnish with the grated carrot, tomato quarters and lime slices. Serve at once, with naan bread, if you like.

COOK'S TIP
For a stronger flavour, brush the fish fillets with the spice mixture an hour or so before you grill them to allow the spices to permeate the flesh.

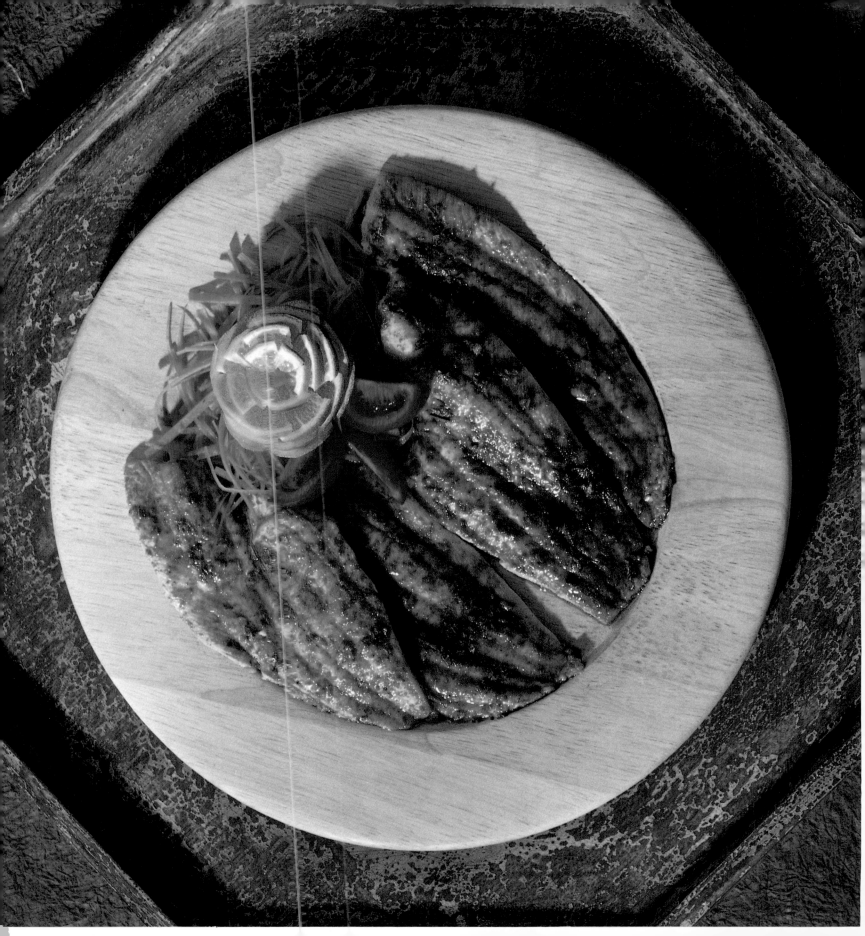

BALTI FISH IN COCONUT SAUCE

U se fresh fish fillets to make this dish if you can, as they have much more flavour than frozen ones. If you are using frozen fillets, ensure that they are completely thawed before cooking.

INGREDIENTS

30ml/2 tbsp corn oil

5ml/1 tsp onion seeds

4 dried red chillies, crumbled

3 garlic cloves, sliced

1 onion, sliced

2 tomatoes

30ml/2 tbsp desiccated coconut

5ml/1 tsp salt

5ml/1 tsp ground coriander

4 flat fish fillets, such as plaice, sole or flounder, about 75g/3oz each

150ml/¼ pint/⅔ cup water

15ml/1 tbsp lime juice

15ml/1 tbsp chopped fresh coriander rice or parathas, to serve

SERVES 4

1 Heat the oil in a deep round-bottomed frying pan or a karahi. Lower the heat slightly and add the onion seeds, dried red chillies, garlic and onion. Cook the mixture for 3–4 minutes, stirring once or twice.

2 Cut a cross on the base of each tomato. Plunge the tomatoes into a bowl of boiling water for 20–30 seconds, then into a bowl of cold water. Peel off the skins, then slice thinly. Add the tomatoes, desiccated coconut, salt and ground coriander to the pan and stir to mix thoroughly.

3 Cut each fish fillet into three pieces. Drop the fish pieces into the onion and tomato mixture and turn them gently until they are well coated.

4 Cook for 5–7 minutes, lowering the heat if necessary. Add the measured water, lime juice and chopped fresh coriander and cook for a further 3–5 minutes, until the water has almost all evaporated. Serve the fish with rice or parathas.

COOK'S TIP

Balti is the name of both a deep, rounded frying pan with two ring handles, and the dish cooked in it. Also known as a karahi, the Balti pan is very similar to a wok, which makes an excellent substitute.

PRAWN AND VEGETABLE KEBABS

This is a light and nutritious dish, excellent served either on a bed of salad leaves, with plain boiled rice or with wholemeal chapatis.

INGREDIENTS

30ml/2 tbsp chopped fresh coriander
5ml/1 tsp salt
2 green chillies, seeded
    and chopped
45ml/3 tbsp lemon juice
30ml/2 tbsp vegetable oil
12 king prawns, cooked and peeled
1 courgette, thickly sliced
1 onion, cut into 8 chunks
8 cherry tomatoes
4 baby sweetcorn
mixed salad leaves, to serve

SERVES 4

COOK'S TIP

If you are using wooden or bamboo skewers, soak them in cold water before use to prevent them from scorching.

1. Place the chopped coriander, salt, green chillies, lemon juice and oil in a food processor or blender, and process for a few seconds until blended.

2. Transfer the coriander mixture to a mixing bowl and add the prawns. Stir thoroughly to make sure that all the prawns are well coated. Cover the bowl and set aside in a cool place to marinate for about 30 minutes. Preheat the grill to very hot.

3. Turn the temperature of the grill down to medium. Arrange the vegetables and prawns alternately on four skewers. Place the skewers under the preheated grill for 5–7 minutes, frequently basting with any remaining marinade, until the vegetables and prawns are cooked and lightly browned on all sides.

4. Serve the kebabs immediately on a bed of mixed salad leaves.

TANDOORI CHICKEN

A popular Indian chicken dish, which is cooked in a clay oven called a tandoor. Although the authentic tandoori flavour is very difficult to achieve in conventional ovens, this version still makes an exceedingly tasty dish.

INGREDIENTS

4 chicken quarters
175ml/6fl oz/³⁄₄ cup natural yogurt
5ml/1 tsp garam masala
5ml/1 tsp grated fresh root ginger
1 garlic clove, crushed
7.5ml/1½ tsp chilli powder
1.5ml/¼ tsp ground turmeric
5ml/1 tsp ground coriander
15ml/1 tbsp lemon juice
5ml/1 tsp salt
few drops of red food colouring
30ml/2 tbsp corn oil
mixed salad leaves, and lime wedges,
to garnish

SERVES 4

1 Skin and rinse the chicken quarters, then pat dry on kitchen paper. Make two slits in the flesh of each chicken quarter, place in a dish and set aside.

2 Mix together the yogurt, garam masala, ginger, garlic, chilli powder, turmeric, coriander, lemon juice, salt, red food colouring and oil and beat together well.

3 Cover the chicken quarters with the spice mixture and leave to marinate for about 3 hours.

4 Preheat the oven to its hottest setting. Transfer the chicken pieces to an ovenproof dish. Bake in the preheated oven for 20–25 minutes or until the chicken is cooked right through and browned on top.

5 Remove the chicken from the oven, transfer to a serving dish and garnish with the salad leaves, and lime wedges.

CHICKEN IN A CASHEW NUT SAUCE

This chicken dish has a deliciously thick and nutty sauce, and is best served with plain boiled rice. Cashew nuts grow profusely in southern India and are widely used in cooking.

INGREDIENTS

2 onions
30ml/2 tbsp tomato purée
50g/2oz/½ cup cashew nuts
7.5ml/1½ tsp garam masala
1 garlic clove, crushed
5ml/1 tsp chilli powder
15ml/1 tbsp lemon juice
1.5ml/¼ tsp ground turmeric
5ml/1 tsp salt
15ml/1 tbsp natural yogurt
30ml/2 tbsp corn oil
15ml/1 tbsp chopped fresh coriander
15ml/1 tbsp sultanas
450g/1lb skinless, boneless chicken breasts, cut into pieces
175g/6oz button mushrooms
300ml/½ pint/1¼ cups water
15ml/1 tbsp chopped fresh coriander, to garnish

SERVES 4

1 Cut the onions into quarters and place in a food processor or blender. Process for about 1 minute.

2 Add the tomato purée, cashew nuts, garam masala, garlic, chilli powder, lemon juice, turmeric, salt and yogurt and process for a further 1–1½ minutes.

3 Heat the oil in a saucepan and pour in the spice mixture. Fry for 2 minutes, over a medium to low heat. Add the coriander, sultanas and chicken, and stir-fry the mixture for 1 minute.

4 Add the mushrooms, pour in the water and bring to a simmer. Cover the saucepan and cook over a low heat for about 10 minutes. Check that the chicken is cooked through and the sauce is thick. Cook for a little longer, if necessary.

5 To serve, ladle the chicken and its sauce on to a warmed serving dish. Garnish with the chopped coriander.

CHICKEN BIRYANI

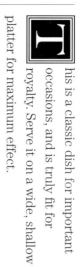

This is a classic dish for important occasions, and is truly fit for royalty. Serve it on a wide, shallow platter for maximum effect.

INGREDIENTS

1.5kg/3–3½lb skinless, boneless chicken breast, cut into large pieces
60ml/4 tbsp biryani masala paste
2 green chillies, chopped
15ml/1 tbsp grated fresh root ginger
2 garlic cloves, crushed
50g/2oz fresh coriander, chopped
6–8 fresh mint leaves, chopped
150ml/¼ pint/⅔ cup natural yogurt
450g/1lb/2½ cups basmati rice, washed
5ml/1 tsp black cumin seeds
5cm/2in cinnamon stick
6 green cardamom pods
vegetable oil, for shallow frying
4 large potatoes, peeled and quartered
300ml/½ pint/1¼ cups skimmed milk
few saffron strands, infused
in milk
salt
30ml/2 tbsp ghee or unsalted butter, plus
extra for shallow-frying,
50g/2oz/½ cup cashew nuts and
50g/2oz/⅓ cup sultanas, to garnish

SERVES 4–6

1 Mix the chicken with the next nine ingredients in a large bowl, cover and leave to marinate for about 2 hours. Place in a large heavy pan and cook gently for about 10 minutes. Set aside.

2 Boil a large pan of water. Add the rice with the cumin seeds, cinnamon stick and cardamom pods; soak for 5 minutes. Drain well. Remove the whole spices.

3 Heat the oil for shallow-frying and fry the potatoes until they are evenly browned on all sides. Drain and set aside.

4 Arrange half of the rice on top of the chicken pieces in the saucepan in an even layer, then make another even layer with the potatoes. Put the remaining rice on top of the potatoes and spread it out to make an even layer.

5 Sprinkle the skimmed milk all over the rice. Make random holes through the rice with the handle of a spoon and pour a little saffron-flavoured milk into each one. Place a few knobs of ghee or butter on the surface of the rice, cover the pan tightly and cook over a low heat for 35–45 minutes.

6 While the biryani is cooking, make the garnish. Heat a little ghee or butter and fry the cashew nuts and sultanas until they swell. Drain and set aside. When the biryani is ready, gently toss the rice, chicken and potatoes together. Transfer to a warmed serving platter, garnish with the nut and sultana mixture and serve immediately.

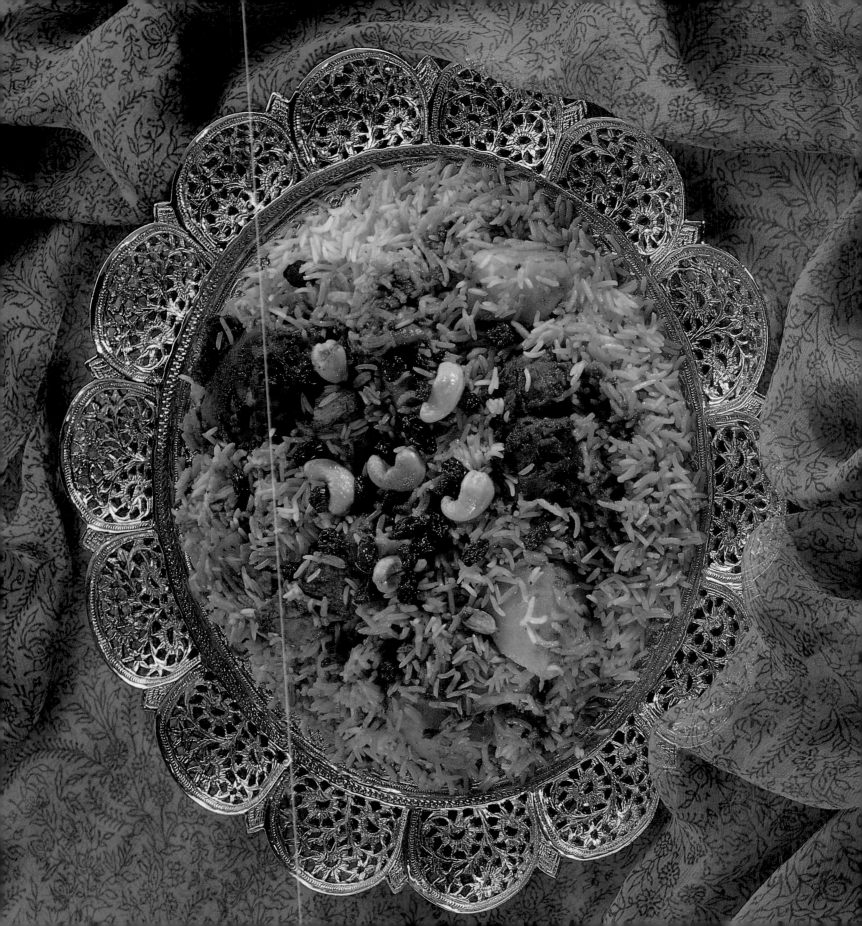

BEEF WITH FRENCH BEANS

French beans both look and taste good with beef in this aromatic sauce. The sliced red pepper used here makes this dish colourful and adds a delicious, sweet touch.

INGREDIENTS

275g/10oz fine French beans, cut into
2.5cm/1in pieces
30ml/2 tbsp vegetable oil
1 onion, sliced
5ml/1 tsp grated fresh root ginger
1 garlic clove, crushed
5ml/1 tsp chilli powder
6.5ml/1¼ tsp salt
1.5ml/¼ tsp ground turmeric
2 tomatoes, peeled and chopped
450g/1lb beef, cubed
1.2 litres/2 pints/5 cups water
1 red pepper, sliced
15ml/1 tbsp chopped fresh coriander
2 green chillies, chopped
wholemeal chapatis, to serve (optional)

SERVES 4

1 Cook the French beans in a saucepan of boiling salted water for 5 minutes, then drain and set aside.

2 Heat the oil in a large saucepan and fry the onion until it turns golden brown.

3 Mix together the ginger, garlic, chilli powder, salt, turmeric and chopped tomatoes. Spoon this mixture into the onion and stir-fry for 5–7 minutes.

4 Add the beef and stir-fry for 3 minutes more. Pour in the measured water, bring to the boil and lower the heat. Cover and cook for 45–60 minutes, stirring the beef occasionally, until most of the water has evaporated and the meat is tender.

5 Add the French beans to the pan and stir well. Finally, add the sliced red pepper, fresh coriander and green chillies and cook, stirring constantly, for a further 7–10 minutes. Serve hot with wholemeal chapatis, if you like.

LAMB KORMA

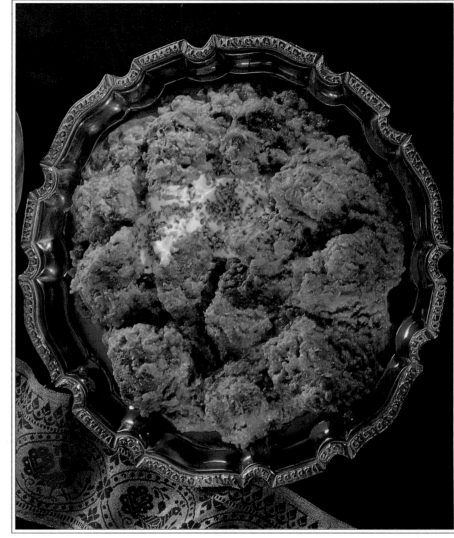

Kormas can be very hot indeed but this one is mild, creamy and aromatic. It comes from the kitchens of the Nizam of Hyderabad.

INGREDIENTS

15ml/1 tbsp sesame seeds
15ml/1 tbsp white poppy seeds
50g/2oz/½ cup blanched almonds
2 green chillies, seeded
6 garlic cloves, sliced
5cm/2in piece fresh root ginger, sliced
1 onion, finely chopped
45ml/3 tbsp ghee or vegetable oil
6 green cardamom pods
5cm/2in cinnamon stick
4 cloves
900g/2lb lean lamb, cubed
5ml/1 tsp ground cumin
5ml/1 tsp ground coriander
300ml/½ pint/1¼ cups double cream
2.5ml/½ tsp cornflour
salt and ground black pepper
roasted sesame seeds, to garnish

SERVES 4–6

1 Heat a heavy-based frying pan and dry-fry the sesame seeds, poppy seeds, almonds, chillies, garlic, ginger and onion. Cool, then grind finely in a food processor.

2 Heat the ghee or oil in the frying pan. Fry the cardamom, cinnamon and cloves until the cloves swell. Add the lamb, cumin and coriander. Stir in the prepared paste. Season to taste. Cover and cook for about 1–1¼ hours, until the lamb is almost done.

3 Remove the pan from the heat. Mix all but 15ml/1 tbsp of the cream with the cornflour. Gradually stir into the lamb mixture. Reheat gently, without boiling and serve, garnished with the sesame seeds and the reserved cream.

STUFFED AUBERGINES WITH LAMB

Minced lamb and aubergines go really well together. This is an attractive dish, using different coloured peppers in the lightly spiced stuffing mixture.

INGREDIENTS

2 aubergines
30ml/2 tbsp vegetable oil
1 onion, sliced
5ml/1 tsp grated fresh root ginger
5ml/1 tsp chilli powder
1 garlic clove, crushed
1.5ml/¼ tsp ground turmeric
5ml/1 tsp salt
5ml/1 tsp ground coriander
1 tomato, chopped
350g/12oz lean leg of lamb, minced
1 green pepper, seeded and
    roughly chopped
1 orange pepper, seeded and
    roughly chopped
30ml/2 tbsp chopped fresh coriander
½ onion, sliced decoratively, 2 cherry
tomatoes, quartered, and fresh coriander
    sprigs, to garnish
green salad or rice, to serve (optional)

Serves 4

1 Preheat the oven to 180°C/350°F/Gas 4. Halve the aubergines lengthways and scoop out most of the flesh and discard. Place the aubergine shells in a lightly greased ovenproof dish.

2 Heat 15ml/1 tbsp of the oil in a large saucepan and fry the onion for about 5 minutes, stirring occasionally, until golden brown. Gradually stir in the ginger, chilli powder, garlic, turmeric, salt and ground coriander. Add the tomato, lower the heat and stir-fry for 4–5 minutes.

3 Add the minced lamb and continue to stir-fry over a medium heat for 7–10 minutes, stirring and turning until the lamb is browned. Add the peppers and fresh coriander to the mixture and stir well.

4 Spoon the lamb mixture into the aubergine shells and brush the edges of the shells with the remaining oil. Bake for 20–25 minutes until cooked through and browned on top. Garnish with the onion, tomatoes and coriander sprigs. Serve with a salad or plain boiled rice, if wished.

SPICED OKRA WITH ALMONDS

Long and elegantly shaped, it's not surprising these vegetables are commonly called "lady's fingers". Native to tropical Africa, they are very popular in India and Arab countries.

Serves 2–4

INGREDIENTS

50g/2oz/¹⁄₂ cup blanched almonds, chopped
25g/1oz/2 tbsp butter
225g/8oz okra
15ml/1 tbsp sunflower oil
2 garlic cloves, crushed
2.5cm/1in piece fresh root ginger, grated
5ml/1 tsp cumin seeds
5ml/1 tsp ground coriander
5ml/1 tsp paprika
300ml/¹⁄₂ pint/1¹⁄₄ cups water
salt and ground black pepper

1 In a shallow flameproof dish, fry the almonds in the butter until they are lightly golden. Remove from the pan with a slotted spoon and drain on kitchen paper.

2 Using a sharp knife, trim the tops of the okra stems and around the edges of the stalks. The pods contain a sticky liquid which oozes out if they are prepared too far in advance, so trim them just before cooking. Heat the oil in the pan, add the okra and fry, stirring constantly with a wooden spoon, for 2 minutes, until the okra starts to soften.

3 Add the garlic and ginger, and fry gently for 1 minute, then add the cumin seeds, coriander and paprika and cook for another 1–2 minutes, stirring all the time.

4 Pour in the measured water. Season generously with salt and pepper, cover the pan and simmer for about 5 minutes until the okra feels just tender when pierced with the tip of a sharp knife. Stir the mixture occasionally.

5 Finally, stir in the fried almonds and serve the dish piping hot.

POTATOES WITH RED CHILLIES

T he quantity of red chillies used here may be too fiery for some palates. For a milder version, either seed the chillies or use a roughly chopped red pepper instead.

SERVES 4

INGREDIENTS

12–14 baby new potatoes, peeled and
halved if large
30ml/2 tbsp vegetable oil
2.5ml/½ tsp crushed dried red chillies
2.5ml/½ tsp white cumin seeds
2.5ml/½ tsp fennel seeds
2.5ml/½ tsp crushed coriander seeds
15ml/1 tbsp salt
1 onion, sliced
1–4 fresh red chillies, chopped
15ml/1 tbsp chopped fresh coriander

1 Put the new potatoes into a saucepan of boiling salted water and cook for 10–12 minutes until tender but still firm. Remove from the heat and drain.

2 Heat the oil in a deep frying pan, then turn down the heat to medium. Add the dried chillies, cumin, fennel and coriander seeds with the salt. Fry for 30–40 seconds.

3 Add the onion. Fry until golden brown. Add the potatoes, fresh chillies and fresh coriander. Cover and cook over a very low heat for 5–7 minutes. Serve hot.

SPICY CABBAGE

A n excellent accompaniment, this cabbage dish is very versatile and can even be served as a warm side salad or cold with a selection of cold meats. Try red cabbage for a change.

INGREDIENTS

50g/2oz/4 tbsp margarine or butter
2.5ml/½ tsp white cumin seeds
3–8 dried red chillies, to taste
1 small onion, sliced
225g/8oz/2½ cups shredded cabbage
2 carrots, grated
2.5ml/½ tsp salt
30ml/2 tbsp lemon juice

SERVES 4

1 Put the margarine or butter into a saucepan and heat until melted. Add the cumin seeds. Crumble in the dried chillies and fry, stirring, for about 30 seconds.

2 Add the onion to the pan and fry for about 2 minutes. Add the cabbage and carrots and stir-fry for a further 5 minutes, or until the cabbage is soft.

3 Finally, stir in the salt and lemon juice. Taste for seasoning, then transfer to a warmed serving dish and serve immediately.

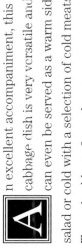

SWEET POTATO AND CARROT SALAD

This salad has a sweet-and-sour flavour, and can be served warm as part of a meal. Offer larger helpings if serving as a main course.

INGREDIENTS

1 sweet potato
2 carrots, cut into thick diagonal slices
3 tomatoes
8–10 iceberg lettuce leaves, shredded
75g/3oz/½ cup canned chick-peas, drained
15ml/1 tbsp walnuts, 15ml/1 tbsp sultanas and 1 small onion, cut into rings, to garnish

FOR THE DRESSING

15ml/1 tbsp clear honey
90ml/6 tbsp natural yogurt
2.5ml/½ tsp salt
5ml/1 tsp ground black pepper

SERVES 4

COOK'S TIP

Plum tomatoes are the best choice for this recipe as they have a greater ratio of flesh to seeds than most other varieties.

1 Peel the sweet potato and dice it roughly. Put it into a pan of boiling salted water and boil until soft but not mushy. Cover the pan and set aside.

4 Line a glass bowl with the shredded lettuce. Mix together the sweet potatoes, carrots, chick-peas and tomatoes and arrange them in the bowl.

2 Put the carrots into a pan of boiling salted water and cook for just a few minutes, so that they remain crunchy. Add the carrots to the sweet potatoes, drain, and place together in a bowl.

3 Carefully slice the tops off the tomatoes, then scoop out and discard the seeds. Roughly chop the flesh.

5 To make the dressing, mix together the honey, yogurt, salt and pepper and beat together with a fork. Garnish the salad with the walnuts, sultanas and onion rings. Pour the dressing over the salad and toss well. Serve the salad in a separate bowl, if wished.

SPICED SPINACH AND POTATOES

India has over 18 varieties of spinach. If you have access to an Indian or Chinese supermarket, it is well worth looking out for some of the more unusual varieties.

INGREDIENTS

450g/1lb potatoes

60ml/4 tbsp vegetable oil

2.5cm/1in piece fresh root ginger, grated

4 garlic cloves, crushed

1 onion, coarsely chopped

2 green chillies, chopped

2 whole dried red chillies, coarsely broken

5ml/1 tsp cumin seeds

225g/8oz fresh spinach, chopped or 225g/8oz frozen spinach, thawed and drained

salt

2 firm tomatoes, peeled and coarsely chopped, to garnish

SERVES 4–6

1 Cut large potatoes into quarters or, if using small new potatoes, leave them whole. Heat the oil in a frying pan and fry the potatoes until brown on all sides. Remove from the pan and set aside.

2 Pour off the excess oil from the pan, leaving 15ml/1 tbsp. Add the ginger, garlic, onion, green and red chillies and cumin seeds and fry gently until the onion is golden brown.

3 Add the potatoes, season with salt, and stir well. Cook, covered, until the potatoes are tender when pierced with the point of a sharp knife.

4 Add the spinach and stir well to mix with the potatoes. Cook, uncovered, until the spinach is tender and all the excess liquid has evaporated. Garnish with the chopped tomatoes and serve hot.

CAULIFLOWER WITH COCONUT

In this dish, the creamy coconut sauce is the perfect contrast to the spiced cauliflower. Serve as a side dish with roast meats as well as the more traditional Indian dishes.

INGREDIENTS

15ml/1 tbsp plain flour
120ml/4fl oz/½ cup water
5ml/1 tsp chilli powder
15ml/1 tbsp ground coriander
5ml/1 tsp ground cumin
5ml/1 tsp mustard powder
5ml/1 tsp ground turmeric
60ml/4 tbsp vegetable oil
6–8 curry leaves
5ml/1 tsp cumin seeds
1 cauliflower, broken into florets
175ml/6fl oz/¾ cup thick coconut milk
juice of 2 lemons
salt
lime wedges, to garnish

SERVES 4–6

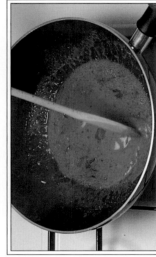

1 Mix the flour with a little of the water to make a smooth paste. Add the chilli, coriander, cumin, mustard, turmeric and salt to taste. Add the remaining water and keep mixing to blend all the ingredients well.

2 Heat the oil in a frying pan and fry the curry leaves and cumin seeds. Add the spice paste and simmer for about 5 minutes. If the sauce has become too thick, add a little hot water.

3 Add the cauliflower and coconut milk. Bring to the boil, cover and simmer until the cauliflower is tender but crunchy. Add the lemon juice, mix well, and serve hot garnished with lime wedges.

43

DRY MOONG DHAL WITH COURGETTES

This is a tasty, colourful accompaniment.

Most dhal dishes tend to be quite liquid but in this one the courgettes provide added body.

INGREDIENTS

175g/6oz/1 cup moong dhal or yellow split peas
2.5ml/½ tsp ground turmeric
300ml/½ pint/1¼ cups water
60ml/4 tbsp vegetable oil
1 large onion, finely sliced
2 garlic cloves, crushed
2 green chillies, chopped
2.5ml/½ tsp mustard seeds
2.5ml/½ tsp cumin seeds
1.5ml/¼ tsp asafoetida
fresh coriander and mint leaves, chopped
6–8 curry leaves
2.5ml/½ tsp sugar
200g/7oz can tomatoes, chopped
225g/8oz courgettes, cut into small pieces
60ml/4 tbsp lemon juice
salt

SERVES 4–6

1 Put the moong dhal or split peas and the turmeric into a saucepan, with the measured water. Bring to the boil, then simmer for 20–30 minutes until the dhal is cooked but not mushy. Drain and reserve both the liquid and the dhal.

COOK'S TIP

Moong dhal is a small teardrop-shaped, yellow split lentil. If you can't find moong dhal, use yellow split peas or small red or green lentils instead. Yellow split peas need soaking in water for about 1–2 hours before cooking.

2 Heat the oil in a frying pan, add the onion, garlic, chillies, mustard and cumin seeds, asafoetida, coriander and mint leaves, curry leaves, sugar, tomatoes and courgettes. Season with salt, and fry over a gentle heat, covered, for 8 minutes until the courgettes are tender but crunchy.

3 Mix the drained dhal and the lemon juice with the courgette mixture in a saucepan. If the dish is too dry, add a little of the reserved cooking liquid. Reheat, transfer to a warmed serving dish and serve.

KITCHIRI

This is the Indian original which inspired the classic breakfast dish – kedgeree. Made with basmati rice and small tasty lentils, this makes an ample supper or brunch dish.

INGREDIENTS

115g/4oz/⅔ cup masoor dhal or
continental green lentils
1 onion, chopped
1 garlic clove, crushed
50g/2oz/¼ cup ghee or butter
30ml/2 tbsp sunflower oil
225g/8oz/1¼ cups easy-cook basmati rice
10ml/2 tsp ground coriander
10ml/2 tsp cumin seeds
2 cloves
3 cardamom pods
2 bay leaves
1 cinnamon stick
1 litre/1¾ pints/4 cups chicken or
vegetable stock
30ml/2 tbsp tomato purée
45ml/3 tbsp chopped fresh coriander
or parsley
salt and ground black pepper

SERVES 4

1 Soak the dhal or lentils in boiling water for 30 minutes. Drain and boil in fresh water for 10 minutes. Drain and set aside.

2 Fry the onion and garlic in the ghee or butter and oil in a large saucepan for about 5 minutes.

3 Add the rice, stir well to coat the grains, then stir in the coriander, cumin, cloves, cardamom pods, bay leaves and cinnamon. Cook gently for 1–2 minutes.

4 Add the dhal or lentils, stock, tomato purée and seasoning. Bring to the boil, then cover and simmer for 20 minutes, until the stock is absorbed and the lentils and rice are just soft. Stir in the coriander or parsley, then check the seasoning. Remove the cinnamon stick and bay leaves, and serve.

LENTILS SEASONED WITH FRIED SPICES

D hal is cooked in every house in India in one form or another. Its warming but unassertive flavour and texture enhances almost any meal

INGREDIENTS

115g/4oz/⅔ cup red split lentils
50g/2oz/⅓ cup bengal gram or yellow split peas,
4 green chillies
5ml/1 tsp ground turmeric
1 large onion, sliced
350ml/12fl oz/1½ cups water
400g/14oz can plum tomatoes, chopped
60ml/4 tbsp vegetable oil
2.5ml/½ tsp mustard seeds
2.5ml/½ tsp cumin seeds
1 garlic clove, crushed
6 curry leaves
2 dried red chillies
1.5ml/¼ tsp asafoetida
salt

SERVES 4–6

1 Place the lentils, split peas, green chillies, turmeric, onion and water in a heavy pan and bring to the boil. Simmer, covered, for 30–40 minutes, until the lentils are soft and almost dry.

2 Mash the lentils. When nearly smooth, add salt to taste, and the tomatoes and mix well. If necessary, thin with hot water.

3 Heat the oil in a small heavy frying pan. Add the mustard seeds, cumin seeds, the crushed garlic, curry leaves, the dried red chillies and asafoetida and fry, stirring, for about 2–3 minutes. Pour the hot spice mixture over the lentils and serve at once.

47

APRICOT CHUTNEY

Chutneys are delicious with curries. In India a good selection of chutneys is often served in tiny bowls to accompany main dishes.

MAKES ABOUT 450G/1LB

INGREDIENTS

450g/1lb/3 cups dried apricots, finely diced

5ml/1 tsp garam masala

275g/10oz/1⅔ cups soft light brown sugar

5ml/1 tsp grated fresh root ginger

75g/3oz/½ cup sultanas

5ml/1 tsp salt

475ml/16fl oz/2 cups malt vinegar

400ml/14fl oz/1⅔ cups water

1 Put the apricots, garam masala, sugar, ginger, sultanas, salt, vinegar and water into a saucepan and mix together.

2 Bring to the boil, then turn down the heat and simmer for 30–35 minutes, stirring occasionally.

3 When the chutney has thickened to a fairly stiff consistency, transfer to small sterilized glass jars and leave to cool. This chutney should be stored in the fridge.

COOK'S TIP

For a hotter chutney, you could add up to 5ml/1 tsp chilli powder. Dried peaches may be used instead of dried apricots – or a mixture of the two.

HOT LIME PICKLE

A good lime pickle not only enhances any meal, it also increases the appetite and aids digestion. If you cannot find mustard oil, use vegetable oil.

INGREDIENTS

25 limes
225g/8oz salt
50g/2oz ground fenugreek
50g/2oz mustard powder
150g/5oz chilli powder
15g/½oz ground turmeric
600ml/1 pint/2½ cups mustard oil
5ml/1 tsp asafoetida
25g/1oz yellow mustard seeds, crushed

MAKES ABOUT 450G/1LB

1 Cut each lime into eight pieces and remove any pips. Place the limes in a large sterilized heatproof glass bowl. Add the salt and toss well. Cover and leave in a warm place for 1–2 weeks until the limes become soft and turn a dull brown.

2 In a small bowl, mix together the fenugreek, mustard powder, chilli powder and turmeric, add to the limes and turn with a wooden spoon until they are thoroughly coated. Cover and leave to stand in a warm place for a further 2–3 days.

3 Heat the oil in a large frying pan and fry the asafoetida and mustard seeds. When the oil reaches smoking point, pour it over the limes. Mix well, cover with a clean dish towel and leave in a warm place for about 1 week before serving.

49

SAFFRON AND CARDAMOM RICE

There are two main ways of cooking rice: one in which all the water is absorbed by the rice and the other where the surplus water is drained, getting rid of any starch from the rice. This recipe uses the second method. Try serving this with Spiced Okra with Almonds.

/

SERVES 6

INGREDIENTS

450g/1lb/2⅔ cups basmati rice
750ml/1¼ pints/3 cups water
3 green cardamom pods
2 cloves
5ml/1 tsp salt
2.5ml/½ tsp crushed saffron strands
45ml/3 tbsp semi-skimmed milk

1 Wash the rice at least twice and place it in a saucepan with the water. Add the cardamon, cloves and salt to the saucepan. Bring to the boil, cover, lower the heat and simmer for about 10 minutes.

2 Meanwhile, place the saffron and milk in a small pan and warm. (Alternatively, put the saffron and milk in a cup and warm for 1 minute in a microwave.)

3 To test whether the rice is ready, use a slotted spoon to lift out a few grains and press them between your index finger and thumb. They should feel soft on the outside but still a little hard in the middle. If the rice is ready, remove the pan from the heat, and carefully drain the rice through a sieve. Rinse out the pan.

4 Return the rice to the pan and pour the saffron and milk over the top. Cover with a tight-fitting lid and place the pan over a medium heat for 7–10 minutes.

5 Remove the pan from the heat and leave the rice to stand, still covered, for a further 5 minutes before serving.

Add the rice and stir for about 1 minute, then pour in the water and bring to the boil. Lower the heat to medium, cover and cook for 12–15 minutes. Leave the rice to stand, covered, for 5 minutes before serving.

COOK'S TIP

Rice should be cooked in a pan with a tight-fitting lid. This prevents any steam from escaping and ensures that the rice cooks evenly.

Gradually add the tomatoes, pepper, ginger, garlic, chilli powder, coriander, potato, salt and peas, and stir-fry over a medium heat for 5 minutes.

ACCOMPANIMENTS

TOMATO RICE

T his delicious dish can be served as an accompaniment or as a lunch or supper dish. It goes well with fish.

INGREDIENTS

30ml/2 tbsp corn oil
2.5ml/½ tsp onion seeds
1 onion, sliced
2 tomatoes, peeled and sliced
1 orange or yellow pepper, seeded and sliced
5ml/1 tsp grated fresh root ginger
1 garlic clove, crushed
5ml/1 tsp chilli powder
30ml/2 tbsp chopped fresh coriander
1 potato, diced
7.5ml/1½ tsp salt
50g/2oz/⅓ cup frozen peas
400g/14oz/2⅓ cups basmati rice, washed
750ml/1¼ pints/3 cups water

SERVES 4

Heat the oil in a large saucepan and fry the onion seeds for about 30 seconds. Add the sliced onion and fry gently for about 5 minutes until softened.

QUICK BASMATI AND NUT PILAFF

light and fragrant basmati rice from the foothills of the Himalayas cooks perfectly using this simple pilaff method. Use your favourite nuts – even unsalted peanuts are good, although almonds or cashews are more exotic, and pistachios add colour and flavour.

INGREDIENTS

225g/8oz/1¼ cups basmati rice

15–30ml/1–2 tbsp sunflower oil

1 onion, chopped

1 garlic clove, crushed

1 large carrot, coarsely grated

5ml/1 tsp cumin seeds

10ml/2 tsp ground coriander

10ml/2 tsp black mustard seeds (optional)

4 cardamom pods

1 bay leaf

475ml/16fl oz/2 cups chicken or vegetable stock or water

75g/3oz/½ cup unsalted nuts

salt and ground black pepper

chopped fresh coriander and fresh coriander sprig, to garnish

Serves 4–6

1 Put the rice in a sieve and wash under cold running water. Transfer the rice to a bowl, add fresh water and soak for about 30 minutes. Drain thoroughly in a sieve.

2 Heat the oil in a large shallow pan, add the onion, garlic and carrot and fry gently for about 5 minutes. Add the rice to the pan with the cumin seeds, ground coriander, black mustard seeds, if using, cardamom pods and bay leaf. Cook for about 1–2 minutes more, stirring the rice and spices, until the rice is thoroughly coated with the spice mixture.

3 Pour in the chicken or vegetable stock or water, and season well. Bring to the boil, cover, lower the heat and simmer very gently for about 10 minutes.

4 Remove the pan from the heat without lifting the lid – this helps the rice to firm up and cook further. Leave to stand for about 5 minutes until small steam holes appear in the centre. Discard the cardamom pods and bay leaf.

5 Stir in the nuts and check the seasoning. Sprinkle with chopped coriander and add a fresh coriander sprig, to garnish.

PARATHAS

P arathas are a richer, softer and flakier variation of chapatis, but they require a longer preparation time, so plan your menu well ahead.

INGREDIENTS

350g/12oz/3 cups atta (wholemeal flour), plus extra for dusting

50g/2oz/½ cup plain flour

2.5ml/½ tsp salt

30ml/2 tbsp ghee

water, to mix

10ml/2 tsp ghee, melted

MAKES 12–15

1 Sift the flours and salt into a mixing bowl. Make a well in the centre and add the ghee. Rub in till the mixture resembles breadcrumbs. Slowly add enough water to make a soft but pliable dough. Cover and leave to rest for an hour.

2 Divide the dough into 12–15 portions and cover. Roll out each to a 10cm/4in round. Brush each round with a little of the melted ghee and dust with atta. Make a straight cut from the centre to the edge. Lift a cut edge and form the dough into a cone.

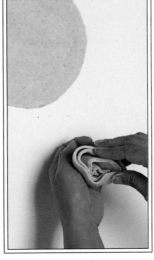

3 Flatten the cone into a ball, then roll out the dough to an 18cm/7in round. Heat a griddle and cook the parathas one at a time, brushing round the edges with the remaining ghee, until golden brown on each side. Serve hot.

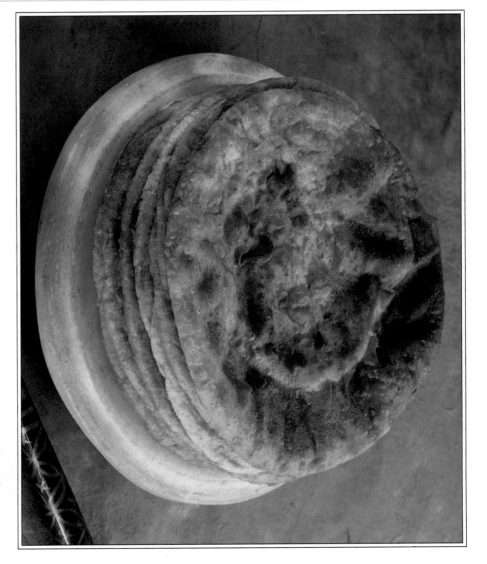

NAAN BREAD

Traditionally, this flat leavened bread from northern India is baked in a tandoor or clay oven, though grilled naans look just as authentic.

INGREDIENTS

450g/1lb/4 cups plain flour
5ml/1 tsp baking powder
2.5ml/½ tsp salt
10ml/2 tsp sugar
10ml/2 tsp easy-blend dried yeast
210ml/7fl oz/scant 1 cup hand-hot milk
150ml/¼ pint/⅔ cup natural
yogurt, beaten
1 egg, beaten
60ml/4 tbsp melted ghee
flour, for dusting
chopped fresh coriander and onion seeds,
to sprinkle
ghee, for greasing
edible silver sheets, to serve (optional)

MAKES 6–8

1 Sift the flour, baking powder and salt into a large bowl. Stir in the sugar and easy-blend dried yeast. Make a well in the centre and add the milk, natural yogurt, egg and melted ghee. Gradually incorporate the flour mixture to make a pliable dough.

2 Knead the dough for about 10 minutes. Place in a bowl, cover tightly and keep in a warm place until the dough doubles in size. To test, push a finger into the dough – it should spring back. On a floured surface roll out the dough to a 5mm/¼in thickness.

3 Preheat the oven to 200°C/400°F/Gas 6. Roll out 6–8 slipper-shaped naans, about 25 × 15cm/10 × 6in tapering to about 5cm/2in. Sprinkle with the coriander and onion seeds. Bake on greased trays for 10–15 minutes. Serve hot, with silver, if using.

55

KULFI

In India *kulfi-wallahs* (ice cream vendors) have always made *kulfi*, and continue to this day, without using modern freezers. *Kulfi* is packed into metal cones sealed with dough and then churned in clay pots until set. This method works extremely well in an ordinary freezer.

SERVES 4–6

INGREDIENTS

3 × 400ml/14fl oz cans evaporated milk
3 egg whites, whisked until peaks form
350g/12oz/2¼ cups icing sugar
5ml/1 tsp ground cardamom
15ml/1 tbsp rose-water
175g/6oz/1½ cups pistachios, chopped
75g/3oz/½ cup sultanas
75g/3oz/¾ cup flaked almonds
8 glacé cherries, halved

1 Remove the labels from the cans of evaporated milk and lie the cans in one large, or two small heavy-based saucepans with tight-fitting lids. Fill the pan with water to reach three-quarters of the way up the cans. Bring to the boil, cover the pan, and simmer for about 20 minutes. When cool, remove from the pan and chill for 24 hours.

2 Open the cans and pour the evaporated milk into a large chilled bowl. Whisk until it doubles in volume, then fold in the whisked egg whites and the icing sugar.

3 Gently fold in the cardamom, rose-water, pistachios, sultanas, almonds and glacé cherries. Cover the bowl with clear film and leave in the freezer for 1 hour.

4 Remove the ice cream from the freezer and mix well with a fork to break up any ice crystals that have formed around the edge. Transfer to a freezer container and return to the freezer to freeze completely. Remove the ice cream from the freezer 10 minutes before serving to soften a little. Scoop into a chilled bowl to serve.

KHEER

Both Muslim and Hindu communities prepare this rice dessert, which is served at mosques and temples. It also features at weddings and banquets.

Serves 4–6

INGREDIENTS

15ml/1 tbsp ghee
5cm/2in cinnamon stick
175g/6oz/1 cup soft brown sugar
115g/4oz/²⁄₃ cup coarsely ground rice
1.2 litres/2 pints/5 cups milk
5ml/1 tsp ground cardamom
50g/2oz/¹⁄₃ cup sultanas
25g/1oz/¹⁄₄ cup flaked almonds
edible silver sheets, to serve (optional)

1 In a heavy-based saucepan, melt the ghee, then add the cinnamon stick and sugar and fry for 5–8 minutes until the sugar begins to caramelize. Reduce the heat immediately this happens.

2 Add the rice and half of the milk. Bring to the boil, stirring constantly to prevent the milk boiling over. Reduce the heat and simmer until the rice is cooked, stirring frequently with a wooden spoon.

3 Add the remaining milk, cardamom, sultanas and almonds, and leave to simmer until thickened, stirring to prevent the kheer from sticking to the pan. Serve hot or cold, decorated with silver, if using.

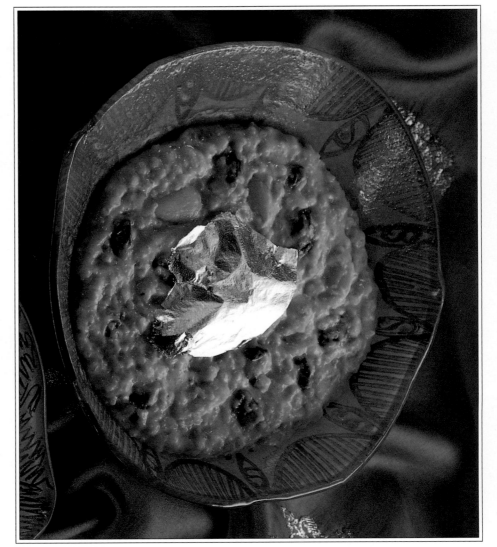

58

FRUIT SALAD

This is a very appetizing and refreshing salad, with a typically Indian combination of citrus fruits seasoned with salt and pepper. It provides the perfect ending to a large meal.

INGREDIENTS

115g/4oz seedless green and black grapes

225g/8oz can mandarin segments, drained

2 large oranges, peeled and segmented

225g/8oz can grapefruit segments, drained

1 honeydew melon, scooped into balls

½ watermelon, scooped into balls

1 mango, peeled and sliced

juice of 1 lemon

2.5ml/½ tsp sugar

1.5ml/¼ tsp freshly ground cumin seeds

salt and ground black pepper

SERVES 6

1 Place the grapes, mandarins, oranges, grapefruit, honeydew and watermelon balls and mango slices in a large serving bowl and add the lemon juice. Toss gently.

2 In a small bowl, combine the sugar, cumin seeds and salt and pepper to taste, then sprinkle over the fruit. Mix gently, chill thoroughly and serve.

MANGO SORBET WITH MANGO SAUCE

After a spicy meal, this makes a most refreshing dessert. Mango is said to be one of the most ancient fruits cultivated in India, having been brought by the god Shiva for his wife, Parvathi.

SERVES 4–6

INGREDIENTS

900g/2lb mango pulp
2.5ml/½ tsp lemon juice
grated rind of 1 orange and 1 lime
4 egg whites, whisked until peaks form
50g/2oz/¼ cup caster sugar
120ml/4fl oz/½ cup double cream
50g/2oz/⅓ cup icing sugar

COOK'S TIP

To prepare mango pulp, cut each mango lengthways on both sides of the stone, then slice the remaining mango from the stone. Make a lattice of cuts through each piece, cutting through the flesh but not the skin. Press the skin, so that the mango looks like a hedgehog, then cut the flesh from the skin. Purée in a blender.

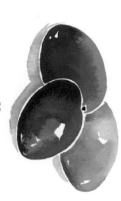

1 In a large chilled bowl, mix 425g/15oz of the mango pulp with the lemon juice and the orange and lime rind.

2 Gently fold in the egg whites and caster sugar. Cover with clear film and place in the freezer for at least 1 hour.

3 Remove the mango mixture from the freezer and beat thoroughly. Transfer to a freezer and freeze fully.

4 To make the sauce, whip the double cream with the icing sugar and the remaining mango pulp. Cover and chill the sauce for 24 hours. Remove the sorbet from the freezer 10 minutes before serving so that it softens slightly. Using a spoon or ice cream scoop, transfer individual servings to chilled bowls and top each with a generous helping of mango sauce.

VERMICELLI PUDDING

Indian vermicelli, made from wheat, has a much finer texture than the Italian variety. It is readily available from Asian shops as *sevijan*.

INGREDIENTS

115g/4oz fine vermicelli
1.2 litres/2 pints/5 cups water
2.5ml/½ tsp saffron strands
15ml/1 tbsp sugar
15ml/1 tbsp each shredded fresh coconut
or desiccated coconut, flaked almonds,
chopped pistachios and
sugar, to decorate
60ml/4 tbsp fromage
frais, to serve (optional)

SERVES 4

1 Crush the vermicelli in your hands and place in a saucepan. Pour in the water, add the saffron and bring to the boil. Boil for about 5 minutes.

2 Stir in the sugar and continue cooking until the water has evaporated from the vermicelli. Strain through a sieve, if necessary, to remove any excess liquid.

3 Ladle the vermicelli into a serving dish and decorate with the coconut, flaked almonds, chopped pistachios and sugar. Serve with fromage frais, if wished.

ORANGES WITH SAFFRON YOGURT

After a hot, spicy curry, a popular Indian pudding is simply sliced, juicy oranges sprinkled with a little cinnamon and served with a spoonful of saffron-flavoured yogurt.

INGREDIENTS

4 large oranges
1.5ml/¼ tsp ground cinnamon
150g/5oz/⅔ cup natural yogurt
10ml/2 tsp caster sugar
3–4 saffron strands
1.5ml/¼ tsp ground ginger
15ml/1 tbsp chopped pistachios, toasted
fresh lemon balm or mint
sprigs, to decorate

SERVES 4

1 Slice the bottoms off the oranges so they sit upright on a board. Working from the top of the oranges, cut across the top and down one side. Follow the contours of the orange to reveal the orange flesh beneath the pith. Repeat until all the rind and pith has been removed, reserving any juice.

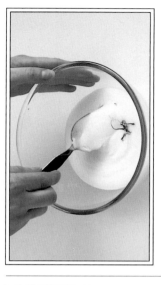

2 Slice the oranges thinly and remove any pips. Place the oranges in a single layer, overlapping the slices, on a shallow serving platter. Sprinkle over the ground cinnamon, then cover and chill until you are ready to serve the dessert.

3 Mix together the yogurt, sugar, saffron and ginger in a bowl and leave to stand for 5 minutes. Spoon into a serving bowl and sprinkle with the nuts. Spoon a little of the yogurt mixture on to each serving and decorate with lemon balm or mint sprigs.

COOK'S TIP
Instead of ordinary oranges, try using clementines or blood oranges.